Origins of the National Navy UDT-SEAL Museum

Origins of the National Navy UDT-SEAL Museum
www.PhocaPress.com/UDT-SEAL-Museum
Copyright © 2019 by Norman Olson

Published by Phoca Press
New York, NY 10019
www.PhocaPress.com

Phoca Press publishes works by, for and about Naval Special Warfare. Our mission is to enhance the public's appreciation and understanding of the contributions of the Naval Special Warfare Community through history until today. All rights reserved. This book or parts thereof may not be reproduced in any form, stored in a retrieval system, or transmitted in any form by any means—electronic, mechanical, photographic, recorded or otherwise—without prior written permission of the publisher, except as provided by United States of America copyright law.

ISBN-13: 978-0-9909153-9-3
10 9 8 7 6 5 4 3 2

Origins of the National Navy UDT-SEAL Museum

By
Norman H. Olson
Captain (SEAL) USN, Retired

Tent City

In early 1943, the Navy took over certain sections of the barrier islands off Florida's East Coast and established the U. S. Naval Amphibious Training Base (USNATB), Fort Pierce, Florida. Training included instruction in the operation of all types of landing craft, including LSTs, LSMs, LCTs and on down to LCVPs. Additionally, Naval Beach Battalions, Joint and later Navy Scouts & Raiders (S&Rs), Naval Combat Demolition Units (NCDUs), and the Pacific Underwater Demolition Teams (UDTs) were trained at this location.

Where the Museum stands today, a "tent city" had been quickly constructed in 1943 to serve as the training site for the first Naval Special Warfare commandos.

Metropolis Of The Indian River

Fort Pierce was a quiet town known for its citrus packing and shipping infrastructure before being transformed into a joint Army and Navy training area during World War II.

As a direct result of an agreement between the Chief of Staff, United States Army and Commander in Chief, United States Fleet, a Joint Army-Navy Experimental Testing (JANET) Board was established on 2 November 1943 at USNATB. Its purpose was to coordinate service responsibilities relating to the breaching of beach and underwater obstacles incident to an amphibious landing. Projects of a Navy character were assigned to the Naval Research Demolition Unit (NRDU), and those that were of particular interest to the Army were assigned to the Engineer Board, Fort Pierce Project. Both conducted projects involving experimentation, development and realistic testing of equipment and techniques.

The barrier islands at Fort Pierce, called North Beach and South Beach, were divided by a deepwater inlet that gave passage for ocean going vessels of moderate draft to the local port facilities on the lagoon known as Indian River. South Beach, which had only a dozen or so permanent structures, became a tent city for trainees. It was here that practically all of the conventional amphibious training took place.

North Beach, a wilderness of palmettos, sand flies, and mosquitoes, became the exclusive domain of the S&Rs, NCDUs and the JANET Board. In July 1943, the first NCDU class commenced training under the leadership of LCDR Draper L. Kauffman. In preparing for the training program, Kauffman requested

The Museum grounds, circa 1943, were littered with obstacles used for demolitions training. The Museum has a amassed a collection of these obstacles, and all were recovered from the water and beaches around Fort Pierce.

the Navy S&Rs to compress their own eight-week physical training program into a single week's schedule. It was officially called "Introduction Week," but it has never been called anything but "Hell Week," by the men who have gone through it. Kauffman and his officers went through the first "Hell Week," establishing the precedent which still stands today: Officers and enlisted men demonstrate the same capabilities and endure the same hardships. Overall attrition then was much like today, 65 to 75%.

In April 1944, CDR Kauffman, considered "The Father of Demolition," went on to command the newly formed UDT-5 in the Pacific, participating in the island campaigns of Saipan, Tinian, Pelelieu, Anguar and the Philippines.

To assure plenty of targets for blasting by the NCDUs, Seabee Detachment 1011 on South Beach made concrete and steel duplicates of enemy underwater beach obstacles and planted them in the waters off North Beach. The cycle of

This vintage postcard from Fort Pierce shows that training in 1943 set the standard for future generations of Naval Special Warfare operators. Rubber boat exercises remain a staple in SEAL selection training.

A Naval Combat Demolition Unit consisted of an officer and five enlisted men. This group from Class #1 poses in front of the tent city in Fort Pierce before shipping out in 1943.

Seabees fabricating obstacles and NCDU men blowing them up went on continuously until the war's end in 1945.

Before the base was closed in 1946, some 140,000 men, 3,500 of whom were NCDUs, had seen some sort of training here. After the base was closed, the area returned to normal. With the rapid post World War II de-militarization and economic growth, there were soon no signs or anything else to let the tourists and new settlers know that Fort Pierce was once the site of a vital Navy base during World War II.

NCDU men conducting rock portage, which required them to work together as a team to get their rubber boat and equipment from one side of the jetty to the other. This training evolution is still conducted today; albeit under more austere conditions in Basic Underwater Demolition / SEAL Training in Coronado, CA.

The Idea Is Born

It was not until 1981 that this training area came back to life in the memories of several vintage UDTs who held a reunion in Fort Pierce. Bob Pfister, a local resident and former member of UDT-15 coordinated the reunion. He invited several community officials to participate, including Tom Kindred of the St. Lucie Parks and Recreation Department and Dick Schmidt of the Chamber of Commerce.

The jetties where World War II commandos once trained became a playground for tourists, as this 1973 post from Fort Pierce shows. Of the vast military base in the area, almost nothing remained.

The enthusiasm of the once-young frogmen was infectious, so much so that it encouraged the community officials to commence discussing the need to:

1. Pursue community support to preserve the memories of the Navy men
2. Let the public know the role played by the community in the war effort
3. Honor the service of the men who trained at the USNATB.

After months of discussion, it soon became apparent that a war museum of some kind would serve this purpose. An informal committee was established to decide on a theme and to acquire a site. The committee was comprised of a loose confederation of 15-20 volunteers led by Schmidt, Kindred, Larry Adams a friend of many whom had served in UDT, and three other locals who were former Navy frogmen, Al Stankie, Dan Dillon and Hal Aschenbrenner.

The site in mind was a building on a parcel of land on North Beach where the NCDUs had conducted much of their training. However, the County had given this land to the State after the bureaucratic struggle for an oceanfront recreational park.

In the seventies, when treasure hunting was in full swing along the Treasure Coast, the State of Florida built a museum on this property to display gold pieces and artifacts salvaged from sunken Spanish galleons. However, this museum, along with one other further north on Florida's East Coast, were not to last, as the northern most one was broken into and robbed. Even though the loot was eventually recovered, the treasures were moved to Tallahassee for safekeeping and both museums were closed. The facilities were returned to the county.

Coming Aboard

Retired U.S. Navy SEAL Captain and Founding Director of the future UDT-SEAL Museum Norm Olson recalls the trial and tribulations in getting the museum established:

With the former treasure museum site now under local control, it was hoped that the County Commission would finance the operation of the World War II Museum,.Those appeals were ultimately unsuccessful.

It was about this time that I was contacted to help move things forward. With my tentative acceptance to establish the Museum and

Founding Director Captain (SEAL) Norman Olson, USN, Ret.

Captain Olson signed on to turn an abandoned structure on a Fort Pierce beach into a world-class museum, befitting the Naval Special Warfare legacy.

serve as its Founding Director, the Museum Committee felt the Commissioners would look more favorably upon providing financial aid.

In January 1985, the Museum Committee presented me to the Commissioners with the request that they again consider providing financial aid to the Museum. As a result of that visit, the position of Director was established under the St. Lucie County Historical Commission, with an agreed upon nine-month salary of $8,000, plus $2,600 for the Museum's utilities and housekeeping expenses.

I officially came aboard on 1 February 1985 and was given the awesome task of completing the Museum in nine months, so that it could be dedicated on Veterans Day 1985.

Captain Olson speaking about the future of the Museum at a NCDU reunion dinner.

The early intent of the Museum Committee was to limit the scope of the Museum to the UDTs of World War II only. Had that been the case, the display of artifacts, documents and photographs would have been severely limited, mainly because the commandos of World War II were truly "Naked Warriors." As such, they had virtually no equipment, except fins, face masks, lead lines, slates, web belts and KA-BAR knives.

NCDU men and their wives and families at a UDT-NCDU reunion.

Additionally, all World War II UDT operations were classified either Secret or Top Secret, thus photographs were virtually non-existent. Moreover, it was years before the classification of most official records were downgraded, and even then many were lost or destroyed. In view of this narrow view, long term funding support would have been extremely limited, and it would have excluded the brotherhood of UDTs and SEALs that followed.

I recognized this conflict early on. Accordingly, my first order of business was to broaden the scope of the Museum to include all post World War II UDTs and SEALs. In concert with this, I played a vital role in establishing the UDT-SEAL Museum Association to replace the UDT Museum Committee.

The constitution and by-laws were written, officers were elected, and the Association was incorporated in the State of Florida as a not-for-profit organization. Its purpose was to foster and perpetuate the UDT-SEAL Museum as a medium of informing and educating the public on the important role of the Navy's NCDUs, UDTs and SEALs. The election of Dick Ward as President, a Korean War-era frogman and local real estate developer, provided a strong business like approach toward the Association's development. During this embryo stage, the importance of close cooperation between Ward and me cannot be understated.

The family of Admiral Draper Kaufman (above circa World War II), who created and led training of Naval Special Warfare operators on Fort Pierce, were deeply involved in establishing the Museum.

Prior to the establishment of the Association, the Historical Commission had anticipated that all artifacts and financial support in the form of memberships,

This series of photographs illustrate the challenges the Museum had in acquiring its first artifacts. Decrepit World War II-era boats were found rotting in various locations. They were rescued, restored, and transported to the Museum for display where you can see them today.

- 20 -

donations and grants would go to the County treasury. Early on, it became patently clear that the UDT-SEAL community at-large was not going to provide funding or loan/donate their personal treasures to a museum in a relatively obscure county in Florida without assurances that they would have a say in its operation. Additionally, several successful former frogmen showed their willingness to donate sizeable sums of money to a privately operated, not-for-profit organization but would not contribute to a government entity.

Moreover, the family of RADM Draper Kauffman had a significant interest in the Museum's future. The Admiral's sister Beth, who had married Prescott Bush, brother of then Vice President Bush, made it clear that they would not donate the Admiral's memorabilia to the Museum, but they would loan it to a privately controlled organization for display in the Museum.

Despite the challenges, the Museum was ready for opening day as promised.

Their concerns were well founded, as most government museums have a reputation for often storing donated artifacts for future barter and many times selling them for profit.

In addition to gaining the full support of active, retired and former Team members from all eras, as well as their families, there were more pragmatic reasons for incorporation of the Association. Foremost, the Naval Historical Center, Washington, DC, The Museum of Florida History, Tallahassee, FL, and the American Historical Foundation, Richmond, VA all recommended it for liability purposes and to serve as the tax-deductible fund raising arm for the Museum.

All of these reasons led to the incorporation of the Association as a not-for-profit organization.

Museum stands ready on the morning of November 10, 1985 to welcome the public.

The development of the Museum during this first nine month period presented a challenge that far exceeded my expectations. During the first few months, I wrote several thousand personal letters to current and former frogmen and SEALs to enlist their financial support, locate former Teammates, procure artifacts, documents and photographs, and identify potential sponsors.

Monetary donations and memberships in the Association were considered paramount in order to reconfigure the inside of the Museum, design and construct display cases, publish a brochure, develop a video presentation, and in general, project an image to the public that would serve the best interests of the Museum, County, State and U.S. Navy.

The Museum was also in dire need of service memorabilia, vintage uniforms, and articles of equipment, war trophies, photographs, documents, and even items that may seem insignificant to a prospective donor. I recognized that there was a natural reluctance to part with artifacts and items of historical significance; however, their contributions were essential if this unique, one-of-a-kind museum were to adequately reflect the history and exploits of the UDT and SEAL Teams.

My pleas notwithstanding, funding was a significant problem throughout, as it relied almost exclusively on memberships, and they were very slow in coming. Moreover, grants and large dollar donations were virtually non-existent. The acquisition of artifacts was also painfully difficult, even with the caveat that they would be on loan to the Association for a period of five years with the option of retrieval at any time during that period.

Dedication

While these challenges were as difficult as any I had encountered in my career, I presented St. Lucie County and the UDT-SEAL community-at-large a completed Museum on Veterans Day 1985. In addition to the actual opening of the Museum, it was equally important that the Dedication Ceremony be conducted with military flair, so that the veterans would be filled with pride and the doubters would have their faith restored.

My first order of business was to arrange for credible Principal Guest Speakers. Commodore "Irish" Flynn, the Community's first Flag Officer, and Mr. Prescott Bush, the former President's brother satisfied that requirement.

While serving as Commanding Officer, NAVPHIBASE, Little Creek, Virginia from 1975-1977, I had established a personal relationship with RADM John O'Connor, Chief of Navy Chaplains (who later became Cardinal of New York City). As a result, he was able to make available Father Edward J. McMahon (who had served previously as a Naval Special Warfare chaplain) to preside over the invocation and benediction.

Unable to arrange for a military band, I called upon the local high school to preside. Since they were unfamiliar with most music associated with military functions, I arranged for the Navy's School of Music in Little Creek to provide the appropriate scores for each instrument.

The Drill Team and Chorus from the Naval Training Center, Orlando was arranged through SKCM Jack Saunders, a long time Teammate and the Center's Naval Special Warfare Recruiting Coordinator.

Through SEAL Master Chief Herschel Davis, another close personal friend and long time sky diving buddy, the Navy Parachute Team was made available to perform at the Ceremony.

And finally, I convinced the Officers of the UDT-SEAL Fraternal Order (now the UDT-SEAL Association) to attend the ceremony, so as to help create an atmosphere of mutual support of both organizations.

Dedication Ceremony

UDT-SEAL MUSEUM
Birthplace of the Navy Frogmen

Sunday the Tenth of November
Nineteen Hundred and Eighty-five
at Twelve Thirty o'clock

Pepper Park
A1A, North Hutchinson Island
Ft. Pierce, Florida

FATHER OF DEMOLITION

REAR ADMIRAL DRAPER L. KAUFFMAN UNITED STATES NAVY (RETIRED) (1911-1979)

Dr. John T. Mason, Jr., Director of Oral History for the Navy Department, summarized the life of Draper L. Kauffman.

This is the record of a naval career that is surely one of the most unusual and most successful. The Admiral graduated from the Academy with the class of 1933 but failed to gain a commission because of defective eyesight. He was employed by the U.S. Lines in New York and very quickly revealed an imagination and drive that brought its own recognition. Yet the advent of war in Europe found him anxious to take part. He enrolled in the American Volunteer Ambulance Corps and served under the aegis of the French Army. Kauffman was taken prisoner by the Germans, spent a brief period in a prison camp, was released to the U.S. Naval Attache in Paris, went to the United Kingdom, enrolled in the Royal Navy Reserve and served a full year as a volunteer in the awesome task of detonating German bombs that failed to explode when dropped over British cities. Then he returned to Washington on leave, was taken up by the U.S. Navy and given a reserve commission after which he was ordered to set up a Bomb Disposal School. From that he went to Fort Pierce and began another school for training what came to be known as the UDTs (Underwater Demolition Teams). Later he commanded a unit of UDTs in the Pacific, taking part in landings on Saipan, Tinian, Iwo Jima and Okinawa. In the post-war period he achieved regular status in the U.S. Navy, enjoyed a series of commands at sea, served as Aide to one Secretary of the Navy and for another set up the OPA (Office of Program Appraisal).

From 1965-68, Rear Admiral Kauffman served as Superintendent of the U.S. Naval Academy. This tour of duty was followed by a tour as Commander, U.S. Naval Forces, Philippines and his career ended as Commander Ninth Naval District with additional duty as Commander Naval Base, Great Lakes. He retired from the Navy in June 1973. He then served for several years as 10th President of the Marion Institute, a Military School in Marion, Alabama. His death came suddenly in Budapest in 1979 during a vacation trip on the Danube River.

He was a dynamic, innovative officer, a humanitarian par excellence — a thoroughly loveable man!

HISTORY

The U.S. Navy entered the underwater demolition arena with the hasty formation of a 17-man detachment that spearheaded the Invasion of North Africa in November 1942. In July 1943, another group of 21 personnel, making up Naval Demolition Unit ONE, responded to an urgent requirement to open channels through Sicily beaches. As the Navy raised its sights for further attacks on both European and Pacific targets, the need for permanent clearance units became apparent, and in the summer of 1943, formalized training of 6-man Naval Combat Demolition Units (NCDUs) commenced at Ft. Pierce, Florida.

In November 1943, while NCDUs were being deployed to both theatres, the amphibious invasion of the Japanese held island of Tarawa was to have a significant impact on the operational concept of the NCDUs. It was during this invasion that waves of Marine-laden assault craft ran aground on an uncharted reef several hundred yards from the beach. While wading ashore, submerged depressions became as lethal as enemy bullets, causing hundreds to drown. This disaster, and the prospective attack on Kwajalein, resulted in the reorganization of the Pacific Fleet NCDUs into 100 men Underwater Demolition Teams (UDTs) and the incorporation of pre-assault hydrographic reconnaissance as an integral part of their demolition clearance mission.

While two UDTs were being organized in Hawaii for the Kwajalein operation scheduled for January 1944, the first NCDUs began arriving in England in preparation for the Normandy Invasion. These NCDUs were expanded to 13-man, joint Army-Navy, "Gap Assault Teams", and on the 6th of June, they were amongst the first to land on Omaha and Utah Beaches. Sustaining overall casualties in excess of 40%, the surviving Omaha Force returned to Ft. Pierce, while the Utah Force redeployed to England to participate in the invasion of Southern France. This was the last NCDU task of the war in Europe and the last major invasion in which demolitioners were not swimmers.

In the Pacific, eight days after the Normandy invasion, Saipan was invaded with five newly formed UDTs paving the way. From this point on UDTs participated in every Pacific Island Campaign from Borneo to Okinawa. By wars end, there were 34 teams with about 3500 men in all. Following demobilization, four teams remained, each at half strength: two in the Pacific and two in the Atlantic.

Several years later during the Korean Conflict, UDTs were once again called into combat. In addition to their classic mission of pre-assault hydrographic reconnaissance and clearance, UDTs conducted night inland demolition raids north of the DMZ against enemy railroads, bridges and tunnels, and served as human minesweepers in harbors and rivers, locating and destroying mines and other underwater obstacles.

The next major conflict that UDT was to participate in was Vietnam, only this time they shared their role with two Sea, Air, Land Teams (SEALs) that had been formed in 1962 in response to President Kennedy's stimulus to expand the Navy's capability in the area of counterinsurgency and unconventional warfare. For over six years, SEALs amassed an impressive combat record by successfully interdicting major Vietcong troop and supply movements. For their size, SEALS emerged as one of the most highly decorated units of the war, including three Congressional Medal of Honor winners.

Some four decades after their inception, the U.S. Navy converted all UDTs to SEAL Teams and merged their mission as one. From their early days in World War II as NCDUs and UDTs, to the present day SEALs, these elite combat units have been in the forefront of every conflict, contingency and national emergency that has faced the Nation. Their history has been one of accomplishment and pride, and the men who lived it have given the UDT and SEAL Teams the undeniable prestige which they enjoy today.

BOARD OF DIRECTORS

UDT-SEAL MUSEUM ASSOCIATION, INC.

Richard D. Ward, President	Roger Cook, Vice-President
Susan Aschenbrenner, Secretary	Marjorie Dillon, Treasurer
Donald D. Griffin	Stuart Sorg
Daniel A. Dillon	John S. Wilbur, Jr.

Harold L. Aschenbrenner

SPECIAL RECOGNITION

The Honorable Bob Graham _____ Governor
State of Florida
The Honorable Havert Fenn _____ Chairman
St. Lucie County Commission
Ms. Lucille R. Rights _____ Chairperson
St. Lucie County
Historical Commission
Mr. Thomas R.L. Kindred _____ Director of Recreation
St. Lucie County

CONSULTING DESIGNER

LCDR Jack F. Macione, USNR (Retired)

PROGRAM

Central High School Band

Arrival of the Official Party

Invocation _____ Commander Edward J. McMahon, USN
Chaplain Corps

Navy Hymm _____ Chorus, Recruit Training Command

National Anthem _____ Central High School Band
Navy Parachute Team

Remarks _____ Ms. Lucille R. Rights, Chairperson
St. Lucie County Historical Commission

Remarks _____ Mr. Richard D. Ward, President
UDT-SEAL Museum Association

Remarks _____ Captain Norman H. Olson, USN (Retired)
Director, UDT-SEAL Museum

Guest Speaker _____ Mr. Prescott S. Bush, Jr.

Guest Speaker _____ Rear Admiral Cathal L. Flynn, USN

Precision Drill _____ Drill Team, Recruit Training Command

Demolitionaire Song _____ Chorus, Recruit Training Command,
Navy Parachute Team

Benediction _____ Commander Edward J. McMahon, USN
Chaplain Corps

Air Show _____ Navy Parachute Team

Ribbon Cutting _____ Official Party

GUEST SPEAKER

MR. PRESCOTT S. BUSH, JR.

Prescott S. Bush, Jr., is the brother-in-law of Rear Admiral Draper L. Kauffman, USN (Retired), and the older brother of the Vice President of the United States. He started Prescott Bush & Company, a business development consulting firm, in January 1985 after 9½ years with Pan American World Airways, and 33 years with Johnson & Higgins, an insurance brokerage firm.

He has been active for 40 years in civic and political affairs. Currently, he is chairman of the Taft Institute for Two Party Government, a trustee of Sacred Heart University and a director of the National Strategy Information Center.

His wife, Elizabeth Kauffman Bush, is the daughter of the late Vice Admiral James L. Kauffman and sister of Rear Admiral Draper L. Kauffman. The Bushs' have three children and three grandchildren. They live in Greenwich, Connecticut.

GUEST SPEAKER

REAR ADMIRAL
CATHAL L. FLYNN
UNITED STATES NAVY

Rear Admiral Flynn assumed command of the Naval Investigative Service Command on 26 August 1985.

He was born in Dublin in 1938, attended school in Ireland, France and Spain, and was graduated from Trinity College with degrees in Arts and Engineering.

He joined the Navy as an Officer Candidate, was commissioned Ensign, USNR, in June 1960, and then completed the Underwater Demolition Team (UDT) Replacement Training Course in Little Creek. Following service as a platoon officer in UDT ELEVEN and SEAL Team ONE, and a tour as SEAL detachment commander with Special Operations Group, Vietnam, he was assigned to OPNAV from 1965 to 1967. He then returned to SEAL Team ONE as Executive Officer and Officer in Charge of the Team's detachment at Nha Be, Vietnam. He commanded UDT TWELVE from January 1968 to July 1969 and had subsequent tours of duty in the Naval Sea Systems Command and on the staff of Commander in Chief U.S. Pacific Fleet. He was Chief Staff Officer of Naval Special Warfare Group ONE from 1977 to 1979, and was assigned to the Assistant Secretary of Defense for International Security Affairs for two years prior to commanding Naval Special Warfare Group ONE from 1981 to 1983. He served in the Joint Special Operations Command from March 1984 to August 1985.

Rear Admiral Flynn is a graduate of the Naval War College's command and staff and post command courses and the National War College. He has an MA in East Asian studies from the American University, Washington, D.C.

Rear Admiral Flynn married Edith Kurtz of Coronado, California, in July 1963. They and their daughter Kathleen (14) live in Burke, Virginia. Their son Patrick (21) and daughter Elizabeth (19) attend the University of California at San Diego.

ACKNOWLEDGEMENTS

Allen Pools, Inc., Port St. Lucie, FL; **Ametek/ORED**, Santa Barbara, CA; **Basic Steel Corporation**, Riverdale, IL; **Buck Knives**, El Cajon, CA; **Central High School**, Ft. Pierce, FL; **Chamber of Commerce**, Ft. Pierce, FL; **Charlton Publications**, Derby, CT; **Chief of Naval Operations**, Washington, D.C.; **Dante's Down the Hatch**, Atlanta, GA; **Defense Audiovisual Command**, Washington, D.C.; **Don Clark Associates**, Ft. Pierce, FL; **Enterprise Leasing Company**, Ft. Pierce, FL; **Ft. Pierce Toyota, Inc.**, Ft. Pierce, FL; **Forth Dimension Design & Decor**, Virginia Beach, VA.

Guardian Systems, Ft. Pierce, FL; **Gung-Ho Magazine**, Broomfield, CO; **Harbor Branch Foundation, Inc.**, Ft. Pierce, FL; **Henderson-Dewey, Realtors**, Wayne, PA; **Historical Association of South Florida**, Miami, FL; **Huston's Office Supplies**, Stuart, FL; **Institute of Diving**, Panama City, FL; **International Diving Museum**, Panama City, FL; **Jensen Beach Kiwanis**, Jensen Beach, FL; **Jetson Appliance Center**, Ft. Pierce, FL; **Knight's Armament Company**, Vero Beach, FL; **Maine Line Video**, Orlando, FL; **Marketing & Management Systems, Ltd.**, Faribault, MN; **Mid-America Recreation**, Moline, IL; **Museum of Florida History**, Tallahassee, FL.

Naval Coastal Systems Center, Panama City, FL; **Naval Experimental Diving Unit**, Panama City, FL; **Naval Historical Center** Washington, D.C.; **Naval Special Warfare Group One**, Coronado, CA; **Naval Special Warfare Group Two**, Little Creek, VA; **Navy Combat Arts Center**, Washington, D.C.; **Navy Office of Information**, Washington, D.C.; **Navy Parachute Team**, Coronado, CA; **Navy Recruiting Command**, Washington, D.C.; **Navy Recruiting Office**, Ft. Pierce, FL; **North Beach Homeowners Association**, Ft. Pierce, FL; **Olin**, East Alton, IL; **Perry Offshore, Inc.**, Riviera Beach, FL; **Promise Printing**, Stuart, FL.

Recruit Training Command, Orlando, FL; **Scubapro**, Huntington Beach, CA; **Seven Seas Construction**, Ft. Pierce, FL; **Smith & Wesson**, Alexandria, VA; **Stickle Steam Specialties**, Indianapolis, IN; **St. Lucie County Historical Commission**, Ft. Pierce, FL; **The American Historical Foundation, Inc.**, Richmond, VA; **The Dive Shop**, Ft. Pierce, FL; **University of South Florida**, Tampa, FL; **Vernon D. Allen Memorial Fund**, Phoenix, AZ; **Ward Realty Corp.**, Jensen Beach, FL; Wenoka Cutlery, West Palm Beach, FL.

SPECIAL ACKNOWLEDGEMENTS

SEAL TEAM FIVE
Coronado, CA

FRATERNAL ORDER OF UDT-SEAL
Virginia Beach, VA

TEXAS EDUCATIONAL ASSOCIATION
Ft. Worth, TX

FOUNDER

Thomas J. & Nancy Clark Ted R. Fielding

BENEFACTOR

Elizabeth R. Bush William W. Saunders

LIFETIME

Peter J. Shea Douglas O. Allred
CDR Thomas L. Hawkins Prescott S. Bush, Jr.

PATRON

Alfred R. Sears Richard P. Jahn
Joseph G. Coyle John S. Wibur, Jr.
George B.M. Stallings Draper L. Kauffman, Jr.

SPONSOR

William Bruhmuller	R.H. Lawry
Roger Cook	Steven B. Nelson
Walter Cooper	Joseph W. Olt, Jr.
Jack F. Couture	John M. Racoosin
Joseph Dimartino	Frank W. Rahn, Jr.
Arthur M. Downs, Jr	George N. Raines, Jr.
Daniel Downs	Glenn W. Reynolds
E.M. Dyal	John C. Roe
Albert Francke, III	Rowena Ruth
Frank E. Goerlich	William P. Salisbury
Richard N. Granger	Robert L. Sanz
Walter E. Hendrick	David L. Schaible
Martin Jacobson	Robert P. Sheehan
James G. Janos	Floyd M. Symons
John H. James	William J. Texido
Cary Kauffman	Lowell K. Williams
Kelsey Kauffman	Arthur R. Wilson
J. Robert Kerrey	Ruth Wolverton
George W. Lavene	George R. Worthington

ARTIFACT CONTRIBUTORS

James Adams
Lawrence Adams
Vernon D. Allen
John Anderson
Layton Bassett
Bud Bechtold
John J. Bell
Christopher O. Brent
Melvin Borror
Steven Bourecksry
William Bruhmuller
Elizabeth R. Bush
R. J. Castro
Raymond A. Cole
Thomas C. Crist
Christine Cromwell
Dr. Harold W. Culver
Lou De Lara
John A. Devine
Donald Donath
Howard Dore
John D. Dumich
John Durham
William Dusseau
E. M. Dyal
Richard N. East
Jerry M. Edwards
John Engraff
Richard D. Faeth
Ted R. Fielding
P.L. Finelli
Lucy A. Folbrecht
William M. Foley
William Garnett
T.J. Glennon
Robert H. Hamilton
Richard D. Harding
Harry Hauck

Cary Kauffman
R. Kozlowski
Martin Jacobson
William Johnson
Frank Lahr
John Lennartz
Donald P. Maury
Timothy McTrusty
Charles Meade
Fredrick Miller
Joseph G. Moretti
H.J. Munson
Joseph Naples
Robert E. Nelson
Steven B. Nelson
James O'Dell
Norman H. Olson
James Ostach
James Pearson
James F. Quiggle
George N. Raines, Jr.
George Ralson
Joseph R. Riordan, Jr.
Paul F. Ryan
Barry T. Sandberg
Jack Saunders
Donald Scully
E. J. Steffen
Virgil R. Stewart
John Thomas
Per Erik Tornblom
Joseph Vogel
F. Walters
Steven Waterman
Robert A. Weems
Harold R. Wilson
Lowell K. Williams
William Woodward
Donald E. Young

DIRECTOR, UDT-SEAL MUSEUM

CAPTAIN NORMAN H. OLSON
UNITED STATES NAVY
(RETIRED)

Captain Norman H. Olson, a native of Providence, Rhode Island, was born on March 14, 1931. He received a Bachelor of Science Degree in Marine Engineering and a Commission in the Naval Reserve in March 1953 from the United States Merchant Marine Academy, Kings Point, New York. Following graduation, and prior to entering the Navy on active duty, he served as a ships officer in the United States Merchant Marine. He holds a current U.S. Coast Guard License as Second Assistant Engineer, Steam Vessel and Third Assistant Engineer, Motor Vessels, any horsepower. Captain Olson was promoted to his present grade in 1972.

He served at sea in USS MOUNTRAIL, USS LENAWEE and USS POCONO, and he commanded Underwater Demolition Team ELEVEN; Naval Operations Support Group, WESTERN PACIFIC DETACHMENT; Maritime Operations Group, USMACV (SOG); Naval Special Warfare Group, ATLANTIC; Naval Amphibious Base, Little Creek, Virginia; and Naval Special Warfare Group TWO. Other assignments included service with Underwater Demolition Team TWENTY-ONE; Naval Operations Support Group, PACIFIC; Naval Inshore Warfare Command, ATLANTIC; the Rapid Deployment Joint Task Force; and the Office of the Chief of Naval Operations. Captain Olson also served in the Arab Republic of Egypt with the Suez Canal Clearance Force as Chief of Staff and subsequently as Commander Task Force SIXTY-FIVE. Prior to his last tour of duty with the U.S. Readiness Command, MacDill Air Force Base, Florida, he served as Chief of Staff, Joint Special Operations Command, Fort Bragg, North Carolina.

On August 1, 1983, he retired from the Navy with over thirty years of commissioned service. Following retirement, and before taking his current position as Director, UDT-SEAL Museum, he served as Security Officer with the Reagan-Bush '84 Campaign Committee.

Captain Olson is a graduate of the Senior Course at the Naval War College, where he was commended for writing an Honors Thesis. He holds a Master of Science Degree in International Affairs from The George Washington University and a Master of Arts Degree in Human Resources Management from Pepperdine University. In 1978, Captain Olson was a recipient of the United States Merchant Marine Academy Alumni Association Professional Achievement Award. The following year, he was accepted into the Hall of Fame of Parachuting, primarily for his contribution as Founder and First Team Leader of the Navy Parachute Team.

He has been awarded the Defense Superior Service Medal, Legion of Merit with Combat "V" and two Gold Stars, Defense Meritorious Service Medal, Meritorious Service Medal, Joint Service Commendation Medal with Combat "V", Navy Commendation Medal with Combat "V" and two Gold Stars, Republic of Vietnam Cross of Gallantry with Gold Star, Republic of Vietnam Medal of Honor (First Class), Arab Republic of Egypt Military Medal of Honor (Second Degree), and numerous other U.S. and Foreign unit citations, unit commendations, and service medals.

Captain Olson is married to the former Barbara Ann Saunders of Baltimore, Maryland and they have four grown children: Christine L., Craig M., Caren S. and Carole J. Olson.

THE UDT-SEAL MUSEUM

Dedicated
November 10, 1985

Preserving the Past to Ensure the Future

UDT-SEAL MUSEUM, P.O. BOX 1117, FT. PIERCE, FL 33454   305-464-FROG

My opening remarks at the Dedication Ceremony, while done in a humorous vein, capture the essence of this formidable task:

"Commodore Flynn, Mr. Bush, Mr. Ward, Ms. Rights, distinguished guests, and most importantly, past members of the Naval Combat Demolition Units and Underwater Demolition Teams, and present members of the Navy's Sea, Air, Land Teams.

"It is my pleasure to welcome many of you back, and all of you, to the birthplace of the navy frogman.

"First and foremost, I want to convey my appreciation to the official party: to Lucille Rights for her full and unconditional support over these past nine months; to Dick Ward for being the primary provider of funds, artifacts and personnel assistance during this embryo stage; to Father Mac, whose close ties with the SEALs in Vietnam will never be forgotten; to Prescott Bush for providing the personal interface with our founder, Rear Admiral Draper L. Kauffman, the "Father of

Demolition;" and to Commodore "Irish" Flynn, a close personal friend for over twenty years, who is not only the senior Naval Special Warfare officer on active duty, but the first and only naval officer to ever attain flag rank from within the UDT-SEAL community. It's a sincere pleasure to have all of you aboard.

"One year ago today, I visited Fort Pierce for the first time to attend the groundbreaking ceremony for this Museum. Following the event and for the next three months, I was courted, led down a primrose path, and finally seduced into becoming the Museum's director. Ladies and gentlemen, I want you to know that it's been a long, lonely, difficult pregnancy.

"As with any prospective blessed event, there were mixed emotions: elation on one hand; grave doubt on the other. Also, there was an immediate craving for support, but all I got was smiles.

"In month two, morning sickness reared its ugly head. Although we all know it's in the mind, anxiety and tension did in fact set in, causing a great deal of heartburn. At this juncture, there appeared to be no relief in sight, and I began to ask myself, "Do I really want this pregnancy?"

"As I came into April, I realized there was no turning back, and I began to accept my fate; however, morning sickness still prevailed, and I now began to feel physically and psychologically uncomfortable. I even started to act a bit crazy, but it received virtually no attention.

"In month four, I began to feel unloved, and I became grouchy, paranoid and downright ugly. I even lashed out at the few friends that I had locally.

"When June rolled around, serious doubt set in, and I began to wonder how I got into this jam in the first place. Intense work, was followed by questions, such as, "Will it be on time?" And "How will it turn out?"

"The following month, I began to feel better, so I took a trip to Norfolk, Virginia to see if this unwed, mother-to-be could obtain a handout. It apparently worked. The trip also cured my nausea, but my heartburn continued, and added to my dilemma was a severe backache from the load I was carrying.

"In August, it became candidly clear that there would be a birth, whether I liked it or not, so I began organizing the nursery, buying a few essentials and enlisting some volunteer help.

"In the eighth month, I really began to feel physically uncomfortable and started to have false labor pains, but this was somewhat compensated for by the baby shower, which bought forth gifts and enough money to take care of expenses.

"As the final month came into full view, there were more false labor pains, insomnia set in, my feet began to swell, and I was having great difficulty just sitting.

"And, as the final hours drew near, and the pain became more excruciating, I still could not help but wonder if it would be on time, or for that matter, whether it would be healthy.

"Ladies and gentlemen, it was a close call, but as you can see, the blessed event took place without serious complications. Although there are a few rough spots, both within and without, I anticipate that in very short order, these wounds will be healed.

"Oh yes — I almost forgot, this beautiful baby does have a name, and a new play toy (unveil the sign mounted on an SDV). Furthermore, its birth is in honor of those who made the ultimate sacrifice for God, country and the United States Navy (unveil the memorial statue).

"In a more serious vein, I owe a great deal, to a great number of people, for permitting me to put this Museum together in record time.

"In February of this year, we had virtually no money, no artifacts and no personnel support; an empty building that had not been maintained for several years; and a great deal of skepticism, both locally and from the museum experts in Miami, Tallahassee and Washington.

"When one considers all of these factors, it's nothing short of a miracle that we have a Museum today. In fact, had you been here at the first of the week, you would have seen absolutely nothing, because there was, in fact, nothing, either inside or out.

"To give you some insight into normal museum development, most evolve over time, and more often than not, as a result of a feasibility study, which doesn't come cheap. I read recently that the City of San Francisco is allocating $73,000 just to determine if a rock-and-roll museum is in the cards for them. We obviously didn't have this luxury, although when the state owned the museum, and was going to take on this task, they had programmed $80,000 and projected five years to completion; we did it in nine months with little over $3,000 of

county operating funds and a great deal of backing from the UDT-SEAL Museum Association.

"I owe all of you a great deal of thanks for having the patience, trust and confidence in me over these past nine months.

"Perhaps to many of you, the purpose of the Museum is crystal clear, but before I step down, I would like to briefly tell you how I see it. This Museum is intended to portray a true image of what the UDT and SEAL Teams are all about.

"It will foster and perpetuate their legacy, by serving as a medium of informing and educating the public on the important role that these teams have played in our nation's history. Our purpose, and bottom line, will be to preserve the past, so as to ensure the future.

"In summary, I would once again remind you of this Museum's short and rocky beginning, and only ask that you be tolerant of what you see and what you may hear. In this regard, I would like to acknowledge Lieutenant Commander Jack Macione, USNR (Retired) for his design expertise. I think you'll be pleased with what you see. If you are, tell me . . . If you are not, tell him.

"As I close, I leave you with a quote from Teddy Roosevelt: "'It is not the critic who counts, not the man who points out how the strong man stumbles, or where the doer of deeds could have done them better.

"The credit belongs to the man who is actually in the arena — who strives – who spends himself — and who at the worst, if he fails, at least he fails by daring, so that his place shall never be with those cold and timid souls who know neither victory nor defeat."

By all accounts, the Dedication Ceremony was a success, with literally hundreds of World War II operators present.

The official party, distinguished guests, and other participants in the ceremony included:

    County Commissioners, St. Lucie County

    Mayor of Fort Pierce

    Commodore Cathal "Irish" Flynn, USN, Commander, Naval Investigative Service Command

    Ms. Lucille R. Rights, Chairperson, St. Lucie County Historical Commission

    Mr. Richard D. Ward, President, UDT-SEAL Museum Association

    Kauffman family

    Mr. Prescott S. Bush, Jr. and his family

    CDR Edward J. McMahon, USN, Chaplain Corps, Naval Air Station, Pensacola, FL

    Chorus, Recruit Training Command, Orlando, FL

Drill Team, Recruit Training Command, Orlando, FL
Navy Parachute Team, Coronado, CA
Central High School Band, Fort Pierce, FL

During the first year of Museum development, the Scouts & Raiders were not considered in the lineage of the NCDUs, UDTs and SEALs, even though the operations they conducted during World War II were closely akin to today's SEALs. Unlike the UDTs, they were totally disestablished after the war, and their history was long forgotten.

From their early days in World War II as NCDUs, S&Rs and UDTs, to the present day SEALs, these elite combat units have been in the forefront of every conflict, contingency, and national emergency that has faced the nation. The purpose of the UDT-SEAL Museum is to foster and perpetuate their legacy, by serving as a medium of informing and educating the public on the important role these Teams have played in our Nation's history. The UDT-SEAL Museum is preserving the past to ensure the future.

In March of 1986, I decided to retire from the position of Founding Director. In late 1993, Andy Andrews, President of the UDT-SEAL Association, asked me to provide a preliminary assessment of the advantages for employing a professionally trained museum person with the requisite qualifications, including education , experience, knowledge, ability and skills. After several months of research and direct contact with professional museum institutions, I submitted a detailed report, "Professional Management of the UDT-SEAL Museum" to the Association President. Beforehand, I asked several museum professionals to read the report, and to a person they told me it was a blueprint for success.

In recognition of my contribution to the establishment of the UDT-SEAL Museum and the UDT-SEAL Museum Association, I was honored in 1998 by the Association with the establishment the "Captain Norman H. Olson Distinguished Achievement Award" to be presented annually to one or more recipients for service to the UDT/SEAL Museum and Naval Special Warfare community. I presented the first award during Muster XIII to Andy Andrews, a World War II Navy frogman and Past President, UDT-SEAL Museum Association. The Achievement Award was subsequently presented each year to: Susan Aschenbrenner, Harold Aschenbrenner, Jim Barnes, Bob Marshall and Marshall Muros.

Also by Captain Olson

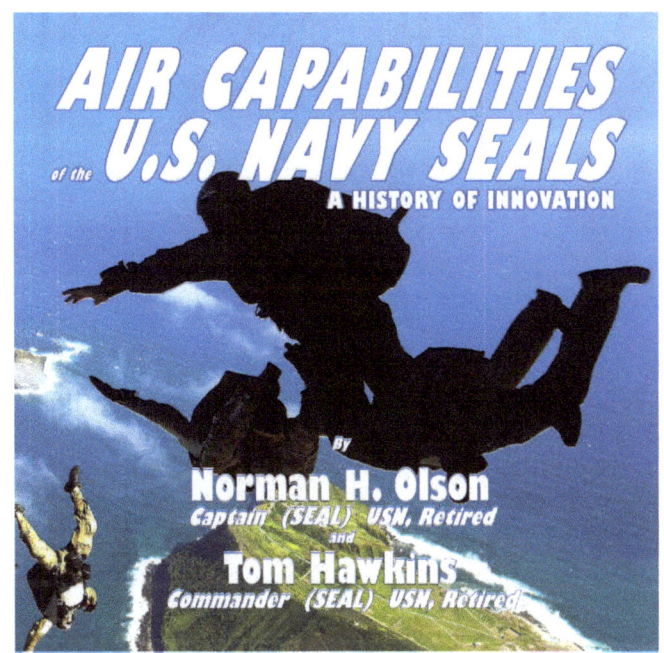

Available at www.PhocaPress.com or
at the National Navy UDT-SEAL Museum

COMMANDER ED MCMAHON, CHAPLIN CORPS, US NAVY

During Award of Presidential Unit Citation to SEAL Team ONE

Dear Father in Heaven,

If I may respectfully say so, sometimes you are a strange God. Though You love all mankind, it seems You have special preferences, too. You seem to love those men who can stand alone, who face impossible odds, who challenge every bully and every tyrant -- those men who know the heat of loneliness of a Calvary.

Possibly You cherish men of this stamp because You recognize the marks of your only Son in them. Since this unique group of men known as SEALS (FROGMEN) know Calvary and suffering, teach them now the mystery of the Resurrection - that they are indestructible, that they will live forever because of their deep faith in You.

And when they do come to Heaven, may I respectfully warm You, dear Father, they also know how to celebrate. So please be ready for them when they insert under your pearly gates.

About the Author
Captain (SEAL) Norman H. Olson, U.S. Navy (Retired)

Captain Olson, a U.S. Merchant Marine Academy alumnus, graduated from what is now called Basic Underwater Demolition/SEAL in East Coast Class 15 in 1955. Six months later, he was designated officer-in-charge of the first detachment of 15 frogmen to attend the U.S. Army's Basic Airborne and Jumpmaster Course at Fort Benning, GA.

In 1959, after serving in UDT-21 for four years, he returned to civilian life. After a period of reflection, he returned to active duty serving at sea as a line officer.

In 1963, Lieutenant Commander Olson took command of UDT-11 and deployed to Southeast Asia and Vietnam where his team conducted combat operations. During the same period, he formed and led the UDT Para-Team (West) that subsequently became the U.S. Navy Parachute Demonstration Team Leap Frogs. In 1967-68, he commanded the U.S. Naval Advisory Detachment Vietnam, where he planned and conducted Maritime Special Operations.

After serving in Vietnam, Commander Olson was assigned as Chief of Staff, Naval Special Warfare Group, ATLANTIC, and in a collateral duty capacity, he formed and led the UDT-SEAL Para-Team (East) that. The team subsequently adopted the name Chuting Stars.

He then graduated from the Naval War College, serving in the Pentagon, and then was deep selected to the rank of Captain. His follow-on assignments included Chief of Staff for Operations, Naval Inshore Warfare Command, ATLANTIC, the first Navy SEAL to command a Major Short Insulation, the Naval Amphibious Base Norfolk, Commodore, Naval Special Warfare Group, TWO, and he ended his Navy career as the first Chief of Staff of the newly formed Joint Special Operations Command. Captain Olson retired in 1983 and worked in the private sector for 16 years. Among his civilian accomplishments, he was the Founding Director of the National Navy UDT/SEAL Museum (now Director Emeritus).

In 2005, at age 74, with 2,200 jumps in his log book, Captain Olson fulfilled the last phase of his parachuting career. He made his 4,000th freefall jump on March 14, 2011, his 80th birthday, and participated in a clean 30-way formation, completed at 9,000 feet. He was recognized for attaining 60-hours in freefall, and being inducted into the Jumpers Over Eighty Society (JOES). At the drop zone, he was irreverently referred to as the "Sky Fossil!"

Captain Olson is a life-long member of the U.S. Parachute Association (#307), License C-1998 and D-1062, and has ratings as a USPA Jumpmaster, Rigger, and Instructor. He has qualifications in the military airbornes of the Republics of Greece, Germany, Vietnam and Thailand.

www.ingramcontent.com/pod-product-compliance
Lightning Source LLC
Chambersburg PA
CBHW061146010526
44118CB00026B/2884